I ♥ XMAS!

An Odd Squad book about the joys of Christmas!

ℛℛ
RAVETTE PUBLISHING

**THE ODD SQUAD and all related characters © 2006
Created by Allan Plenderleith**

www.allanplenderleith.com

First Published in 2006
Reprinted 2007
Ravette Publishing Limited
Unit 3, Tristar Centre, Star Road, Partridge Green,
West Sussex RH13 8RA

Printed and bound in Belgium

ISBN: 978-1-84161-262-1

The family's after-dinner board game ends in the usual fashion.

As the light came on, Santa realised he wasn't the only fat person in the room with a big beard.

Billy's Dad taught him NOT to go hunting for his Christmas presents.

Eating 15 million mince pies in one night
can really block you up.

It had been a while since Lily had got her hands on a man's bulging sack.

To get rid of annoying carol singers,
Jeff feeds the dog a dodgy curry.

As she approached the cash machine, Maude sensed she had taken out too much money over Christmas.

The cat would soon wipe that smug grin off the goldfish's face - his present from Santa had finally arrived!

Maude finally finishes washing up the Christmas dishes.

Jeff had mistakenly left his guests alone with his 'Christmas Hits' CD on the stereo.

Suddenly Santa regretted the day he'd replaced the reindeer with Windows XP.

Jeff decides to start his Christmas shopping.

Maude had asked Jeff to get her something for Christmas with diamonds.

Once again, the elf's trip to Alton Towers ends in misery.

At Christmas, Jeff meets a fellow sufferer.

Not everyone thinks global warming
is a bad thing.

Mum wondered if anyone thought the Christmas pud was a tad heavy this year.

Rudolf likes a girl with something to hold onto.

To save money at Christmas, Maude puts the kids' stockings on a hot wash.

Jeff's dog learns why dogs should never sit down on icy pavements.

The dog finally gets what he'd always wanted for Christmas.

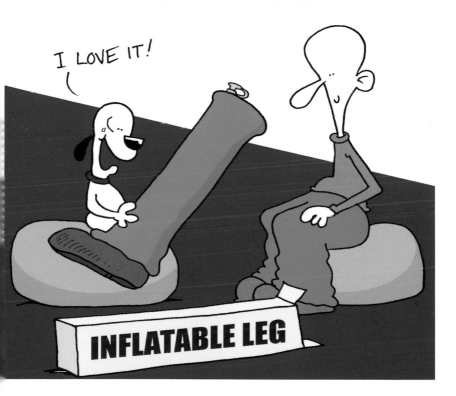

Santa noticed kids' Christmas lists have changed over the years.

Santa realises it had been a mistake to have replaced Blitzen with Leroy the donkey.

At the office Christmas party, Maude likes to let her hair down.

It was so cold Alf could see
Lily's nipples.

At Christmas, Jeff likes to leave the newspaper boy a tip.

As a Christmas treat, Jeff always puts some nuts in Maude's stockings.

The dog liked to keep warm by hiding
under his old friend Jasper.

Typical - you spend all that time picking the kid a nice gift and they end up playing with the box.

Although Santa had forgotten his packed lunch,
Rudolf kindly gave him a chocolate log.

Jeff gets another rubbish jumper for Christmas.

Santa knew Rudolph was healthy because
he had a lovely wet nose.

Maude was so excited! She could see Santa's sack coming down the chimney.

Unfortunately, the mince pie Billy had put out for Santa proved to be one too many.

Santa awoke on Christmas morning groggy and with a headache - but the worst part was yet to come...

Suddenly Santa wished he hadn't
come back for his hat.

Uh oh! The kid had woken up.
'Thank God for red wallpaper,' thought Santa.

Unfortunately, Santa's eyesight wasn't what it used to be.

Suddenly the 3 wise men realise their new sat-nav system was on the blink.

Every year, Santa dreads delivering presents to the Single Women's Foundation.

Jeff prepares in advance for receiving his Christmas presents.

Maude's Christmas wish came true:
she got a small bum.

Sadly, things had changed since
Jeff was a lad.

Unable to find a carrot for the snowman's nose,
Billy grabbed something from his Mum's room.

Maude had actually asked her mum to treat her to a 'spa' day for Christmas.

Maude explained to Billy that Santa had stolen all the chocolate treats from the tree during the night.

After Christmas dinner, everyone was completely stuffed.

Dad received the perfect gift from the kids for Christmas.

Jeff had a feeling he had eaten too much turkey over Christmas.

Maude surprises the postman on Christmas day with something warm and fluffy.

With the kids no longer content with a sixpence in the Christmas pud, Maude had to up the ante.

Suddenly Maude regretted giving the dog
the 3 week old leftover turkey.

This Christmas, Jeff was determined to get a lie in.

Caring Lily always made sure the birds had enough food over winter.

Maude was shocked: it was Christmas day and Jeff had actually laid the table.

Other ODD SQUAD books available ...

		ISBN	Price
The Best of Jeff and Maude (new-Oct 07)		978-1-84161-294-2	£9.99
The Odd Squad's Disgusting Book for Boys	(hardback)	978-1-84161-273-7	£7.99
The Odd Squad's Big Poo Handbook	(hardback)	978-1-84161-168-6	£7.99
The Odd Squad's Sexy Sex Manual	(hardback)	978-1-84161-220-1	£7.99
The Odd Squad Butt Naked		978-1-84161-190-7	£3.99
The Odd Squad Gross Out!		978-1-84161-219-5	£3.99
The Odd Squad's Saggy Bits		978-1-84161-218-8	£3.99
The REAL Kama Sutra		978-1-84161-103-7	£3.99
The Odd Squad Volume One		978-1-85304-936-1	£3.99
I Love Poo!	(hardback)	978-1-84161-240-9	£4.99
I Love Sex!	(hardback)	978-1-84161-241-6	£4.99
I Love Wine!	(hardback)	978-1-84161-239-3	£4.99
I Love Beer!	(hardback)	978-1-84161-238-6	£4.99
I Love Dad!	(hardback)	978-1-84161-252-2	£4.99
I Love Mum!	(hardback)	978-1-84161-249-2	£4.99
The Odd Squad's Little Book of Booze		978-1-84161-138-9	£2.99
The Odd Squad's Little Book of Men		978-1-84161-093-1	£2.99
The Odd Squad's Little Book of Oldies		978-1-84161-139-6	£2.99
The Odd Squad's Little Book of Poo		978-1-84161-096-2	£2.99
The Odd Squad's Little Book of Pumping		978-1-84161-140-2	£2.50
The Odd Squad's Little Book of Sex		978-1-84161-095-5	£2.99
The Odd Squad's Little Book of Women		978-1-84161-094-8	£2.99
The Odd Squad's Little Book of X-Rated Cartoons		978-1-84161-141-9	£2.99

HOW TO ORDER: Please send a cheque/postal order in £ sterling, made payable to 'Ravette Publishing' for the cover price of the books and allow the following for post & packing ...

UK & BFPO	70p for the first book & 40p per book thereafter
Europe & Eire	£1.30 for the first book & 70p per book thereafter
Rest of the world	£2.20 for the first book & £1.10 per book thereafter

RAVETTE PUBLISHING
Unit 3, Tristar Centre, Star Road, Partridge Green, West Sussex RH13 8RA

Prices and availability are subject to change without prior notice.